Collins

VOCABULARY
Organizer

Record and review your vocabulary

PETE SHARMA & BARNEY BARRETT

Collins

HarperCollins Publishers
77–85 Fulham Palace Road
Hammersmith
London W6 8JB

First edition 2014

Reprint 10 9 8 7 6 5 4 3 2 1 0

© HarperCollins Publishers 2014

Produced for HarperCollins by:
White-Thomson Publishing Ltd.
0843 208 7460
www.wtpub.co.uk

Editor: Kelly Davis
Layout designer: Kim Williams

ISBN 978-0-00-755193-4

Collins® is a registered trademark of HarperCollins Publishers Limited

www.collinselt.com

A catalogue record for this book is available from the British Library

Printed in China by South China Printing Co. Ltd

MIX
Paper from
responsible sources
FSC™ C007454
www.fsc.org

FSC™ is a non-profit international organisation established to promote the responsible management of the world's forests. Products carrying the FSC label are independently certified to assure consumers that they come from forests that are managed to meet the social, economic and ecological needs of present and future generations, and other controlled sources.

Find out more about HarperCollins and the environment at
www.harpercollins.co.uk/green

Contents

Introduction

While you are at university, you will learn a huge number of new words and expressions. It is important to develop good learning practices in order to use these words appropriately in your speaking and writing.

This introduction will discuss:

- how many words there are in English
- the best way of recording vocabulary
- what 'knowing a word' means
- how to use your learner's dictionary
- and how to use your new *Vocabulary Organizer*.

1 How many words are there in English?

Students often ask this question. Some experts estimate that there are at least a quarter of a million words in English. One reason why it is so difficult to give an exact number is that the total partly depends on how we define 'a word'. For instance, does a word with more than one meaning count as only one word? Should we include different forms (such as *love* and *loves*) as separate words? It has been estimated that a university-educated speaker knows anywhere between 17,000 and 20,000 words, including words (such as *love*) and derivations (such as *loves – loved – loving*).

The words you recognize (but don't use) make up your passive ('receptive') vocabulary; while the words you actually use in speaking and writing make up your active ('productive') vocabulary. We all recognize more words than we use, so our passive vocabulary is larger than our active vocabulary.

That is why this *Vocabulary Organizer* is divided into two sections. Section 1 is for your productive vocabulary – the words and phrases you want to use when you speak and write. Section 2 is for your receptive vocabulary – the words you are happy simply to recognize when you listen and read.

2 What's the best way to record vocabulary?

Students taking a language course, or studying in a foreign language, often write down the new words they learn during classes and lectures. These notes are usually taken chronologically, meaning that the student starts writing the new words at the beginning of the class or lecture and continues to the end. Many students write down each new word, with a translation next to it, in a vocabulary notebook. However, they may later want to find one of these new words in order to use it or revise it. In this situation, a chronological list is no help at all. The notes have usually been written down quickly and briefly, and they are not in any order, which makes it impossible to find a particular word or phrase. For all these reasons, it is a good idea to transfer new words into your *Vocabulary Organizer*.

 Task

Think about how you record vocabulary. How effective is your method? Can you find the words or phrases again? Can you remember how to pronounce them and how to use them? How could you record new words better?

The most effective language learners have a system they use to store new words and make notes about their meanings. Students take in information in different ways, and there are several methods of recording vocabulary. These include:

- Writing down each word chronologically, with the translation next to it
- Writing words in alphabetical groups, as in a dictionary
- Writing words in a diagram, such as a 'word tree' (see below)
- Writing words in lexical sets (groups of words that are related to each other, such as words about pronunciation or technology).

Writing down a word with a translation next to it is useful for some words, such as simple nouns, and it is helpful when you start your studies. However, it is not very effective for key (important) words, or when you progress past intermediate level. Some words are very complex or have several meanings, which cannot be covered by a simple translation.

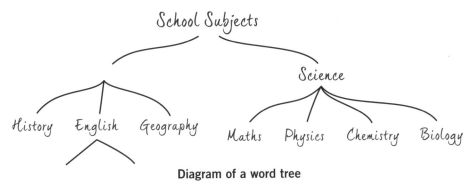

Diagram of a word tree

3   What does 'knowing a word' mean?

'Knowing a word' may include knowing its:

- Meaning or meanings
- Forms
- Pronunciation/Word stress
- Spelling
- Collocation
- Connotation
- Register
- Synonyms and antonyms
- Etymology.

Meaning or meanings

Some words have several different meanings, such as *port*:

A port is a town by the sea, which has a harbour.

A port on a computer is a place where you can attach another piece of equipment, such as a printer.

(Definitions from: *Collins COBUILD Advanced Dictionary of English*, Seventh Edition, 2012)

Forms

Some words have a number of forms, such as: *happy – unhappy – unhappily; politics – politician – apolitical.*

A 'word family' is a group of words that are closely related to each other, such as: *historian – history – historical.*

Pronunciation/Word stress

You can look up the pronunciation of a word in your dictionary. Phonemic script is used to show the pronunciation. Word stress is indicated in the *Collins COBUILD Advanced Dictionary* by underlining the stressed syllable in the phonemic script, so *happy* is written /hæpi/.

Often words have more than one syllable. In the *Collins COBUILD Advanced Dictionary*, the syllables are shown by vertical lines. For example:

> *hap|py*
> *po|li|ti|cian*

Spelling

You can look up the spelling of a word in your dictionary. Plurals of nouns and inflections (the different forms) of verbs are also given. In the *Collins COBUILD Advanced Dictionary*, we give both irregular and regular inflections for every word.

Collocation

Collocations are words that are often used together and thus form strong combinations. For example, some verb–noun collocations of *meeting* are:

- *to attend a meeting*
- *to postpone a meeting*
- *to cancel a meeting*

Connotation

Connotation refers to the feelings connected with a word. These feelings may be positive or negative. For example, the term *freedom-fighter* has a positive connotation; while the word *terrorist* (which may be used by a different speaker to describe the same person) has a negative connotation.

Register

It is good to know if a word has a certain register, such as 'formal' or 'informal'.

There are other labels that can also be used to describe the way certain words are used. These may include:

- Colloquial – used in informal conversation
- Slang – very informal, maybe used by just one group
- Jargon – words that are used by specific groups of professional people (such as information technology jargon)
- ESP – meaning 'English for Specific Purposes'. Sometimes, a word has a restricted use. For example, it may be a word that is only found in legal English (such as *heretofore*) or a word that is only used in technical English (such as *bandwidth*)
- EAP – meaning 'English for Academic Purposes'.

Synonyms and antonyms

It is often helpful to learn a word's synonyms (other words with the same meaning), as well as its antonyms (words with opposite meanings). Taking *decrease* as an example:

- Synonyms would include: *drop* and *fall*
- Antonyms would include: *increase* and *rise*

In the *Collins COBUILD Advanced Dictionary*, synonyms and antonyms are listed.

Etymology

Occasionally, it can be useful to know the origins of a word. For instance, a word could have a Latin root (*insomnia*); it could come from Greek (*democracy*); or it could be a loan word imported from another language such as Hindi (*juggernaut*), Japanese (*karaoke*) or Portuguese (*cashew*).

In the *Collins COBUILD Advanced Dictionary*, there are 'Word links boxes' that focus on word roots, as well as prefixes and suffixes. For example, *geo-* is a prefix meaning 'earth' that is used in words like: *geography*, *geology* and *geopolitical*.

4 How to use your learner's dictionary

Dictionaries are available in several formats, including:

- The book version (paperback or hardback)
- The CD-ROM or DVD-ROM version
- The Internet (online) version
- The smartphone or tablet app.

For information on electronic dictionaries and translators (which may contain bilingual and monolingual versions), see page 184.

 Task
Which format of dictionary or dictionaries do you use? What are the advantages and disadvantages of using a specific type of dictionary?

We usually use a dictionary to look up the meaning of a word. In a bilingual dictionary, this will probably be a translation from your own language. In a monolingual learner's dictionary, the definition will be in English. This type of dictionary uses a restricted number of words to write the definitions – known as the 'defining vocabulary'. The defining vocabulary used in the *Collins COBUILD Advanced Dictionary* is listed at the end of the dictionary.

A learner's dictionary does more than simply provide the definition of a word. The best learner's dictionaries, such as the *Collins COBUILD Advanced Dictionary*, have certain features that can help you use them more effectively. Some of these features are listed below.

Meaning labels

Many words have many different meanings. These are labelled so that you can find the correct one to fit the context in which you have met the word or intend to use it.

 Task
Look up the word *fit* in your dictionary and see how many meanings are listed and how they are labelled.

Example sentences

Example sentences show the context in which the word is most commonly used. These sentences also demonstrate grammatical structures associated with the word. For instance, an example sentence can show you whether a particular verb is followed by another verb in the infinitive or by a preposition and a gerund. Example sentences may also include common collocations associated with the word.

For instance:

*money (n) – We **spent** a lot of **money** on developing the prototype.*
*work (v) – I **work for** a small software company.*

 Task

Look up *money* and *work* in your dictionary and see which other collocations are illustrated in the example sentences.

The *Collins COBUILD Advanced Dictionary* includes 'Word partnership boxes' that highlight common collocations.

Usage labels

Learner's dictionaries also provide guidance on the correct use of words. For example, the register of a word is shown by its label ('formal' or 'informal'), and this will help you use it appropriately. British and American differences in usage, spelling and pronunciation are indicated by codes such as 'BrE' or 'UK' and 'AmE' or 'US'.

 Task

Look up *pavement*, *behaviour* and *laboratory* and see how your dictionary indicates the differences in usage, spelling and pronunciation.

Some learner's dictionaries include boxes highlighting errors commonly made in English or similar words that are frequently confused. The *Collins COBUILD Advanced Dictionary* includes 'Usage boxes' for this purpose.

Word frequency

Your English–English dictionary (monolingual) provides information on frequency (how common a word or phrase is). Knowing how frequent a word is will help you decide in which section of your *Vocabulary Organizer* to store it.

The *Collins COBUILD Advanced Dictionary* uses diamond symbols to show frequency, from three diamonds for 'most frequent' to no diamonds for 'less frequent'. This is how the system works:

◆◆◆	the most frequent words in English
◆◆	fairly frequent words
◆	frequent words
No diamond	less frequent words.

We suggest that you put all the words marked with one or more diamonds in Section 1 (Vocabulary for production). These words are important for your area of study and they will be your 'active vocabulary'. All the words without this symbol are words that you need to recognize but not produce. They are your 'passive vocabulary' and they will go in Section 2 (Vocabulary for recognition).

The *Collins COBUILD Advanced Dictionary* is a general English dictionary so you should bear in mind that there might be a word that doesn't have a frequency marker but should still go in Section 1 of your *Vocabulary Organizer* because it's going to be a common word in your field of expertise.

5 How to use your *Vocabulary Organizer*

Your *Vocabulary Organizer* is divided into two sections. Section 1 is for you to record the vocabulary you need to use – your productive (active) vocabulary. Section 2 is to record the vocabulary you need to recognize – your receptive (passive) vocabulary. When you record new words in your *Vocabulary Organizer*, you should first decide whether you want to store them in Section 1 or Section 2.

Using Section 1

The pages in Section 1 will help you record important information about new words. Section 1 is divided into:

- My word maps
- My new words
- My new phrasal verbs/collocations/idioms and expressions
- My key words.

My word maps

This section of your book will help you record words together in 'concept areas'. It is easier to remember important words if you record them in groups (such as types of fruit, collocations of the word *meeting*, or parts of a car) rather than just alphabetically.

 Task

Create some word maps for concepts that are important to you. Here are some suggested concept areas for general English and English for Special Purposes to get you started:

General: animals/hobbies/photography/music/emotions and feelings
English for Academic Purposes: sociology/culture/art/business and management/law

Two example word maps have been completed (see pages 12 and 13).

The 'Word web boxes' in the *Collins COBUILD Advanced Dictionary* present topic-related vocabulary using text and pictures.

My new words

When you wish to record a new word, add it to this section. There is room to record some useful information about each word and to write in an example phrase or sentence.

My new phrasal verbs/collocations/idioms and expressions

These pages are for recording 'chunks' of language. 'Chunks' are pieces of language that are longer than individual words or compound words (e.g. *computing science*). These can be recorded in the 'My new phrases' section. For example, you can use this section to record:

- Phrasal verbs – *she **puts up with** a lot of*
- Useful 'word partnerships' or 'collocations' – ***ozone layer***
- Idioms, expressions and fixed phrases that you may wish to use – ***the other side of the coin***, *I'd like to...*

For examples of these, see pages 44, 54 and 64.

My key words

Use these pages if a new word is very important, and you wish to record a lot of information about it. You can record details of the word such as collocations, different forms and word stress. Finally, write some examples that are useful for you. You can revisit these pages and update them, adding more information.

See pages 74 and 75 for examples of completed key word pages.

Using Section 2

In this section you can store words alphabetically. Storing vocabulary alphabetically means that the words are easy to access when you want to review them. Remember, these words are only for recognition (rather than production) so you will need to record less information about them.

Your *Vocabulary Organizer* will prove invaluable when it comes to revising vocabulary. This 'recycling' of words and phrases is necessary for them to become part of your everyday vocabulary. You may need to meet and use a new word or phrase as many as eight times before it passes from your short-term memory into your productive vocabulary. You can:

- look at the words you have recorded in Section 1 and see if you can use any of them in an essay or presentation
- use your *Vocabulary Organizer* when you are writing or preparing a talk
- return to the word maps and your key words from time to time, and add more information.

Your *Vocabulary Organizer* will continue to be useful as you progress through your studies.

We hope you enjoy using your *Vocabulary Organizer*.

Pete Sharma and **Barney Barrett**

About the authors

Pete Sharma is currently working as a lecturer in English for Academic Purposes at universities in the UK. He is a prolific ELT author and a well-known conference presenter, having given workshops and keynote speeches around the world on language teaching.

Barney Barrett is an experienced English language teacher and writer based in the UK, where he works for an international Business English training organization. Barney is currently writing and developing learning materials that form part of blended learning English courses.

Section 1

Vocabulary for production

Words I need to be able to say and write

- ◆ My word maps
- ◆ My new words
- ◆ My new phrasal verbs
- ◆ My new collocations
- ◆ My new idioms and expressions
- ◆ My key words

EXAMPLE

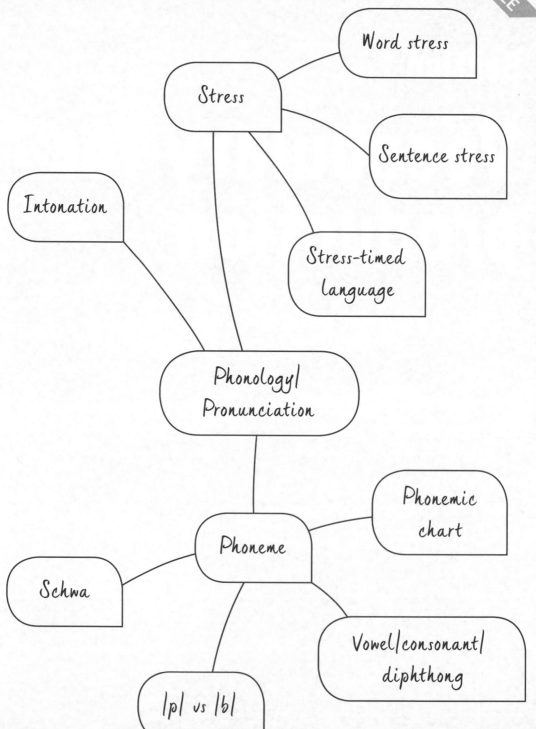

Word stress

Stress

Sentence stress

Intonation

Stress-timed language

Phonology/ Pronunciation

Phoneme

Phonemic chart

Schwa

Vowel/consonant/ diphthong

/p/ vs /b/

M-learning
= mobile learning

Interactive
phonetic chart

Web/websites

Test (online)

e-book

Internet

PLE
= personal learning
environment

DVD-ROM

VLE
= virtual learning
environment

CD-ROM

Technology + language
learning

synchronous
asynchronous

Electronic
translator

Chat (MSN)

WIKI
= Wikipedia

e-mail forum

Podcast

post 'thread'

Blog
= web + log

mp3

iPod
+ broadcast

vodcast
= video podcast

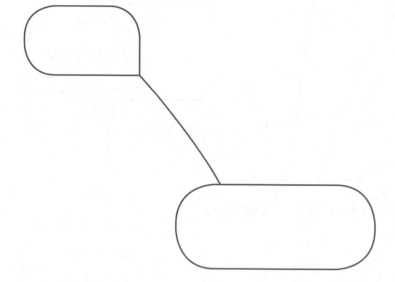

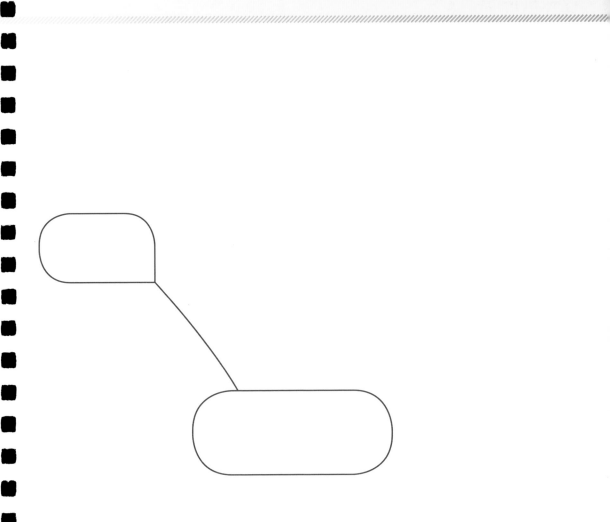

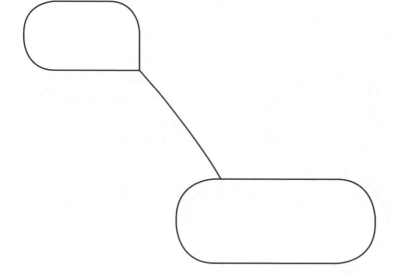

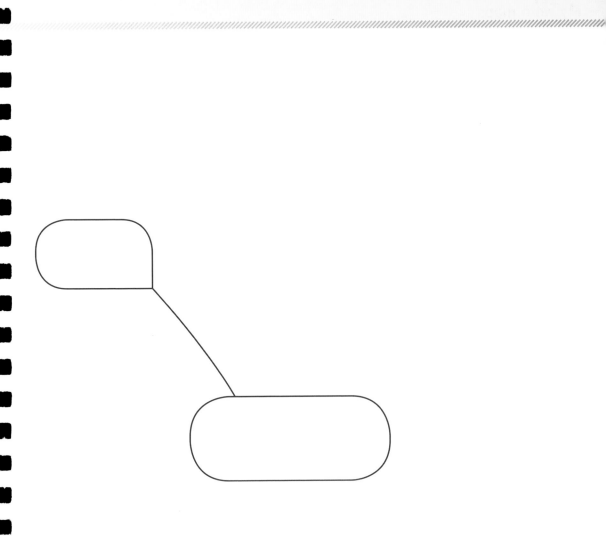

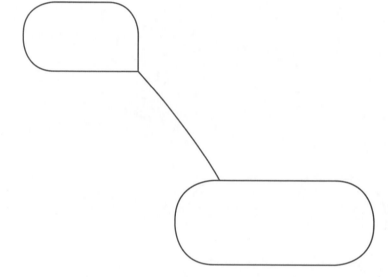

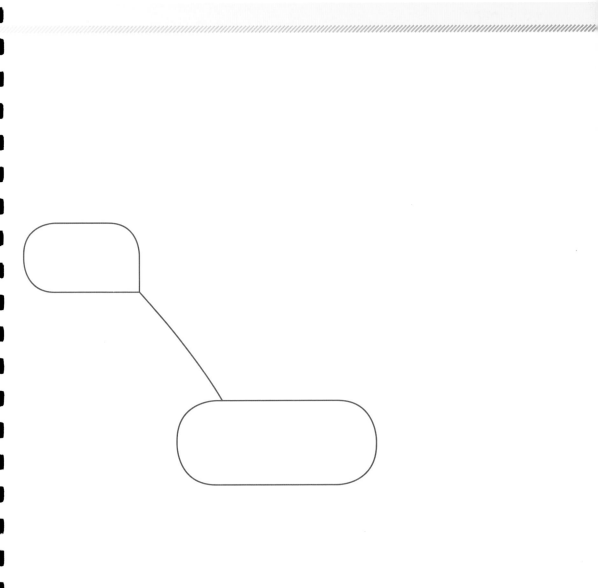

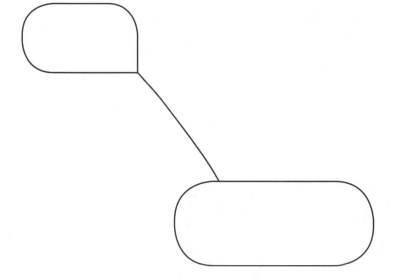

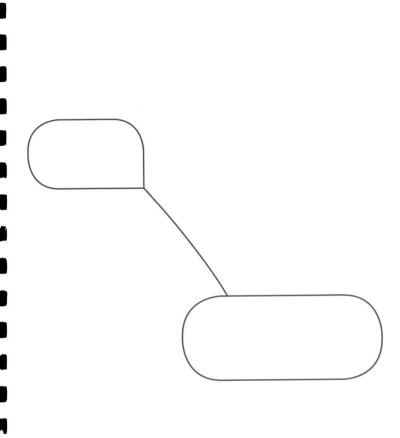

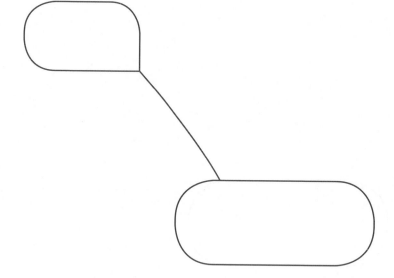

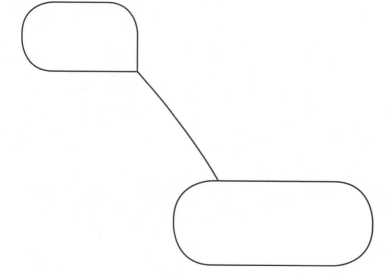

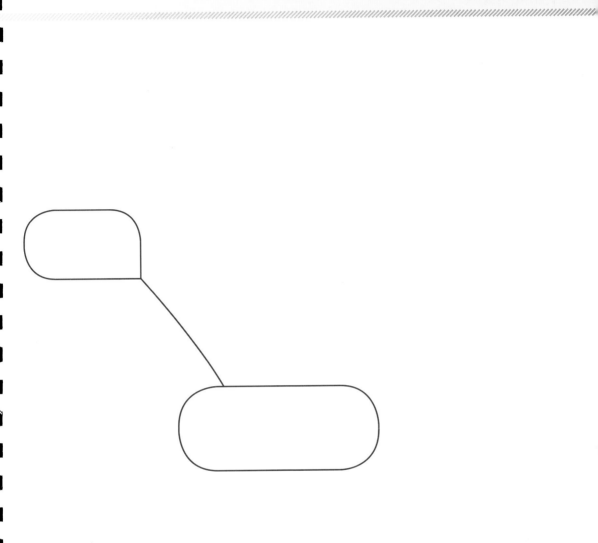

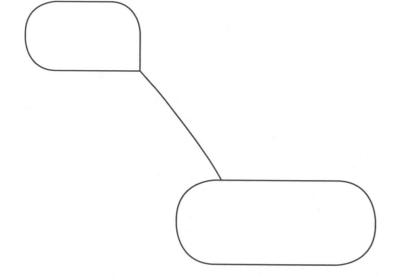

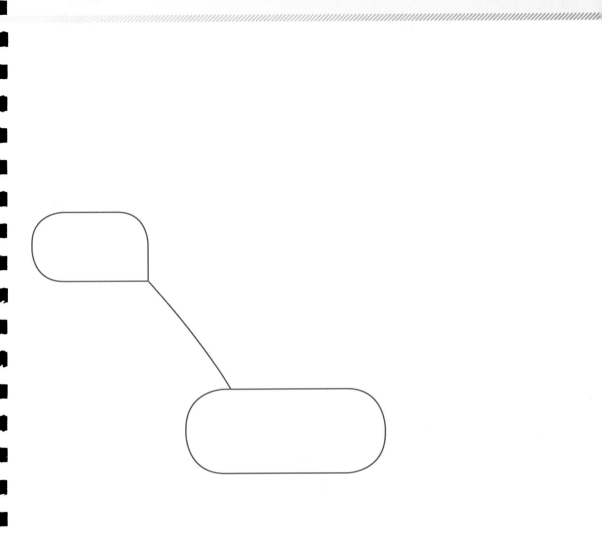

EXAMPLE

Word	Meaning	My example	Translation
fraudulent [law]	being deliberately deceitful or dishonest	The businessman was accused of fraudulent misrepresentation.	
short-termism	someone makes decisions that produce benefit now rather than in the future	The short-termism of government policy is likely to lead to future problems.	

Word	Meaning	My example	Translation
Immer	Always		Always

My new words

Word	Meaning	My example	Translation

Word	Meaning	My example	Translation

My new words

Word	Meaning	My example	Translation

Word	Meaning	My example	Translation

My new words

Word	Meaning	My example	Translation

Word	Meaning	My example	Translation

Word	Meaning	My example	Translation

Word	Meaning	My example	Translation

My new words

Word	Meaning	My example	Translation

Word	Meaning	My example	Translation

My new words

Word	Meaning	My example	Translation

Word	Meaning	My example	Translation

Word	Meaning	My example	Translation

Word	Meaning	My example	Translation

Phrasal verbs	Meaning/translation	My example
put up with	accept something that is not pleasant	I cannot put up with the terrible weather in England, so I might leave.
take up	become interested in and start doing something	Last year, I took up yoga.

Phrasal verbs	Meaning/translation	My example

Phrasal verbs	Meaning/translation	My example

Phrasal verbs	Meaning/translation	My example

My new phrasal verbs

Phrasal verbs	Meaning/translation	My example

Phrasal verbs	Meaning/translation	My example

My new phrasal verbs

Phrasal verbs	Meaning/translation	My example

Phrasal verbs	Meaning/translation	My example

Phrasal verbs	Meaning/translation	My example

Phrasal verbs	Meaning/translation	My example

EXAMPLE

Collocations	Meaning/translation	My example
fulfil a promise	do what you said or hoped you would do	The president fulfilled his promise of announcing a date for the referendum.
reliable data	you can trust this data; also reliable info/source	It is not difficult to get reliable data on childhood diseases in West Africa.

Collocations	Meaning/translation	My example

Collocations	Meaning/translation	My example

Collocations	Meaning/translation	My example

My new collocations

Collocations	Meaning/translation	My example

Collocations	Meaning/translation	My example

My new collocations

Collocations	Meaning/translation	My example

Collocations	Meaning/translation	My example

My new collocations

Collocations	Meaning/translation	My example

Collocations	Meaning/translation	My example

My new idioms and expressions

Idioms and expressions	Meaning/translation	My example
give (someone) the benefit of the doubt	believe something good about someone instead of bad	Because there were no witnesses, the tribunal gave him the benefit of the doubt.
be at a loose end	have nothing to do	Last weekend I was at a loose end, but then I met Jay and we went to town.

Idioms and expressions	Meaning/translation	My example

My new idioms and expressions

Idioms and expressions	Meaning/translation	My example

Idioms and expressions	Meaning/translation	My example

My new idioms and expressions

Idioms and expressions	Meaning/translation	My example

Idioms and expressions	Meaning/translation	My example

My new idioms and expressions

Idioms and expressions	Meaning/translation	My example

Idioms and expressions	Meaning/translation	My example

My new idioms and expressions

Idioms and expressions	Meaning/translation	My example

Idioms and expressions	Meaning/translation	My example

EXAMPLE

Word	Concept area
argument (n)	EAP | essays | debate

Meaning(s)	Form(s)
reason you can use to persuade other people to accept your views	arguable (adj) arguably counter-argument

Collocations

strong \| weak
build an argument
counter-argument
argument essay
win \| lose (an argument)

Pronunciation

Stress: ●●●

Notes

argumentative - this is negative
this is a v. common academic word

My example sentences

My next assignment is an argument essay.

Word	Concept area
economy (the economy)	business / finance

Meaning(s)	Form(s)
relationship between production, trade + money supply	economy (n) economist (person) economic / economical economically (adv) (to economize)

Collocations

handle / run / manage (+ the e.)
stimulate the economy
economy class (fly)

Pronunciation

●●**●**● – economic
●**●**●● – economy

Notes

countable
economic – about money (economic forecast)
economical = good value (Mini = economical car)
NB: <u>two</u> adjectives!

My example sentences

The economy in Japan is in recession.
My dad is an economist.

Word	Concept area

Meaning(s)	Form(s)

Collocations	
	Pronunciation

Notes

My example sentences

Word	Concept area

Meaning(s)	Form(s)

Collocations	
	Pronunciation

Notes

My example sentences

Word	Concept area

Meaning(s)	Form(s)

Collocations

Pronunciation

Notes

My example sentences

Word	Concept area

Meaning(s)	Form(s)

Collocations	Pronunciation

Notes

My example sentences

Word	Concept area

Meaning(s)	Form(s)

Collocations

Pronunciation

Notes

My example sentences

Word	Concept area

Meaning(s)	Form(s)

Collocations

Pronunciation

Notes

My example sentences

My key words

Word	Concept area

Meaning(s)	Form(s)

Collocations

Pronunciation

Notes

My example sentences

Word	Concept area

Meaning(s)	Form(s)

Collocations

Pronunciation

Notes

My example sentences

My key words

Word	Concept area

Meaning(s)	Form(s)

Collocations

Pronunciation

Notes

My example sentences

Word	Concept area

Meaning(s)	Form(s)

Collocations

Pronunciation

Notes

My example sentences

Word	Concept area

Meaning(s)	Form(s)

Collocations

Pronunciation

Notes

My example sentences

Word	Concept area

Meaning(s)	Form(s)

Collocations	
	Pronunciation

Notes

My example sentences

My key words

Word	Concept area

Meaning(s)	Form(s)

Collocations

Pronunciation

Notes

My example sentences

Word	Concept area

Meaning(s)	Form(s)

Collocations	
	Pronunciation

Notes

My example sentences

Word	Concept area

Meaning(s)	Form(s)

Collocations

Pronunciation

Notes

My example sentences

Word	Concept area

Meaning(s)	Form(s)

Collocations	
	Pronunciation

Notes

My example sentences

Word	Concept area

Meaning(s)	Form(s)

Collocations

Pronunciation

Notes

My example sentences

Word	Concept area

Meaning(s)	Form(s)

Collocations	
	Pronunciation

Notes

My example sentences

Word	Concept area

Meaning(s)	Form(s)

Collocations

Pronunciation

Notes

My example sentences

Word	Concept area

Meaning(s)	Form(s)

Collocations	
	Pronunciation

Notes

My example sentences

Word	Concept area

Meaning(s)	Form(s)

Collocations	
	Pronunciation

Notes

My example sentences

Word	Concept area

Meaning(s)	Form(s)

Collocations

Pronunciation

Notes

My example sentences

Word	Concept area

Meaning(s)	Form(s)

Collocations

Pronunciation

Notes

My example sentences

Word	Concept area

Meaning(s)	Form(s)

Collocations	
	Pronunciation

Notes

My example sentences

Word	Concept area

Meaning(s)	Form(s)

Collocations

Pronunciation

Notes

My example sentences

Word	Concept area

Meaning(s)	Form(s)

Collocations	Pronunciation

Notes

My example sentences

Section 2

Vocabulary for recognition (A-Z)

Words I need to be able to understand

Word	Meaning/example
acquit	If someone is acquitted of a crime, it is formally declared that they did not commit it. - John was acquitted at the county court and set free.
attain	If you attain something, you achieve it after a lot of effort. - I'm hoping to attain a first.

Word	Meaning/example

Word	Meaning/example

Word	Meaning/example

Word	Meaning/example

Word	Meaning/example

Word	Meaning/example

Word	Meaning/example

Word	Meaning/example

Word	Meaning/example

Word	Meaning/example

Word	Meaning/example

Word	Meaning/example

Word	Meaning/example

Word	Meaning/example

Word	Meaning/example

Word	Meaning/example

Word	Meaning/example

Word	Meaning/example

Word	Meaning/example

My words for recognition

Word	Meaning/example

Word	Meaning/example

Word	Meaning/example

Word	Meaning/example

Word	Meaning/example

Word	Meaning/example

Word	Meaning/example

Word	Meaning/example

Word	Meaning/example

Word	Meaning/example

Word	Meaning/example

Word	Meaning/example

Word	Meaning/example

Word	Meaning/example

Word	Meaning/example

Word	Meaning/example

Word	Meaning/example

Word	Meaning/example

Word	Meaning/example

Word	Meaning/example

My words for recognition

Word	Meaning/example

Word	Meaning/example

My words for recognition

Word	Meaning/example

Word	Meaning/example

Word	Meaning/example

Word	Meaning/example

Word	Meaning/example

Word	Meaning/example

Word	Meaning/example

Word	Meaning/example

Word	Meaning/example

Word	Meaning/example

Word	Meaning/example

Word	Meaning/example

Word	Meaning/example

Word	Meaning/example

Word	Meaning/example

Word	Meaning/example

Word	Meaning/example

Word	Meaning/example

Word	Meaning/example

Word	Meaning/example

Word	Meaning/example

Word	Meaning/example

Word	Meaning/example

Word	Meaning/example

My words for recognition

Word	Meaning/example

Word	Meaning/example

Word	Meaning/example

Word	Meaning/example

Word	Meaning/example

Word	Meaning/example

Word	Meaning/example

Word	Meaning/example

Word	Meaning/example

Word	Meaning/example

Word	Meaning/example

Word	Meaning/example

Word	Meaning/example

Word	Meaning/example

1 The Academic wordlist

The Academic Word List (AWL) includes words that often occur in academic subjects – particularly in articles and lectures. The list was compiled by Averil Coxhead at the Victoria University of Wellington, New Zealand. It contains 570 word families and is divided into 10 sub-lists. Sublist 1 consists 60 of the most common words in the AWL. Sublist 2 contains the next most frequently used words, and so on.

You don't need to know the AWL by heart, but it is useful to consult it occasionally to ensure that the words you are learning are those that occur frequently in academic contexts. The *Collins COBUILD Advanced Dictionary* contains the AWL.

There are no technical words in the list. You will need to supplement the AWL by noting down any new technical words from your own field of specialist study.

AWL weblink:
www.uefap.com/vocab/select/awl.htm

2 Corpora

A corpus is a 'collection of texts, written or spoken, which is stored on a computer'. It has been described as a 'principled' collection of texts, which means that it represents an area of language, such as 'business English' or 'classroom discourse'.

Collins and the University of Birmingham developed an electronic corpus in the 1980s, called the Collins Birmingham University International Language Database (COBUILD). This corpus became the largest collection of English data in the world, and COBUILD dictionary editors use the corpus to analyse the way people use language.

The Collins Corpus contains 4.5 billion words taken from websites, newspapers, magazines and books published around the world. It also includes spoken material from radio, TV and everyday conversations. All the examples in COBUILD dictionaries are examples of real English, taken from the Collins Corpus.

A concordance enables the user to find out how often, and in what contexts, a word or phrase is used in a corpus.

Online concordance weblink:
www.lextutor.ca/concordancers

3 Electronic dictionaries

Electronic dictionaries are available in several formats: web-based; on CD-ROM and DVD-ROM; and on dictionary apps.

A dictionary on CD-ROM provides an excellent opportunity to listen to a new word. You can click on the audio icon to hear the word in British English or American English. You can also practise your pronunciation by recording the new word, comparing your recording with the original, then re-recording yourself as many times as you wish.

If you have the CD or DVD-ROM version of a learner's dictionary, you can also make use of production tools, such as ready-made word families and a thesaurus (which groups words from the dictionary families, based on their meaning and usage, instead of the alphabetic list used in the main dictionary).

Access the *Collins COBUILD Advanced Dictionary* online at:
www.collinsdictionary.com

This glossary contains some of the more difficult words in the *Vocabulary Organizer*.

antonym The **antonym** of a word is a word that means the opposite.

app An **app** is a computer program that is written and designed for a specific purpose. It is designed for use on a mobile digital device. *The company recently launched a free phone* **app** *that translates conversations while you speak.*

collocation In linguistics, **collocation** is the way that some words occur regularly whenever another word is used.

connotation The **connotations** of a particular word or name are the ideas or qualities that it makes you think of.

corpus A **corpus** is a large collection of written or spoken texts that is used for language research.

countable A **countable noun** is the same as a **count noun**. A **count noun** is a noun such as *bird*, *chair* or *year*, which has a singular and a plural form and is always used after a determiner in the singular.

frequency The **frequency** of an event is the number of times it happens during a particular period of time.

intransitive An **intransitive** verb does not have an object, such as *Last month house prices* **rose**.

phrasal verb A **phrasal verb** is a combination of a verb and an adverb or preposition, such as *shut up* or *look after*, which together have a particular meaning.

synonym A **synonym** is a word or expression that means the same as another word or expression.

transitive A **transitive** verb has a direct object, such as *She* **sent** *me a text*.

uncountable An **uncountable noun** is the same as an **uncount noun**. An **uncount noun** is a noun such as *gold*, *information* or *furniture*, which has only one form and can be used without a determiner.

British English vowel sounds

ɑː	heart, start, calm
æ	act, mass, lap
aɪ	dive, cry, mine
aɪə	fire, tyre, buyer
aʊ	out, down, loud
aʊə	flour, tower, sour
e	met, lend, pen
eɪ	say, main, weight
eə	fair, care, wear
ɪ	fit, win, list
iː	feed, me, beat
ɪə	near, beard, clear
ɒ	lot, lost, spot
əʊ	note, phone, coat
ɔː	more, cord, claw
ɔɪ	boy, coin, joint
ʊ	could, stood, hood
uː	you, use, choose
ʊə	sure, pure, cure
ɜː	turn, third, word
ʌ	but, fund, must
ə	butter, about, forgotten

American English vowel sounds

ɑ	calm, drop, fall
ɑː	draw, saw
æ	act, mass, lap
ai	drive, cry, lie
aiər	fire, tire, buyer
au	out, down, loud
auər	flour, tower, sour
e	met, lend, pen
ei	say, main, weight
eər	fair, care, wear
ɪ	fit, win, list
i	feed, me, beat
ɪər	cheer, hear, clear
oʊ	note, phone, coat
ɔ	more, cord, sort
ɔi	boy, coin, joint
ʊ	could, stood, hood
u	you, use, choose
ʊər	sure, pure, cure
ɜr	turn, third, word
ʌ	but, fund, must
ə	about, account, cancel

Consonant sounds

b	bed	l	lip	v	van	tʃ	cheap
d	done	m	mat	w	win	θ	thin
f	fit	n	nine	x	locks	ð	then
g	good	p	pay	z	zoo	dʒ	joy
h	hat	r	run	ʃ	ship		
j	yellow	s	soon	ʒ	measure		
k	king	t	talk	ŋ	sing		

Letters

These are vowel letters:
a e i o u

These are consonant letters:
b c d f g h j k l m n p q r s t v w x y z

The letter 'y' is sometimes used as a vowel, for example in *shy* and *myth*.

This pronunciation guide is taken from *Collins COBUILD English Usage* (2012).

When two words have a similar or identical sound, it is easy to confuse them and use the correct spelling for the wrong word. Here's a list of sets of words that are easily confused.

accept, except – To **accept** something is to receive it or agree to it. **Except** means 'other than' or 'apart from'.

affect, effect – To **affect** something is to influence or change it. An **effect** is a result something gives, or an impression something makes.

aid, aide – **Aid** means 'help', and to aid somebody is to help them. An **aide** is someone who acts as an assistant to an important person.

allude, elude – To **allude** to something is to refer to it in an indirect way. If something **eludes** you, you can't understand or remember it. If you **elude** something, you dodge or escape from it.

altar, alter – An **altar** is a holy table in a church or temple. To **alter** something is to change it.

ascent, assent – An **ascent** is an upward climb. To **assent** to something is to agree to it, and **assent** means 'agreement'.

aural, oral – Something that is **aural** is to do with the ear or listening. Something that is **oral** is to do with the mouth or speaking.

berth, birth – A **berth** is a bed on a ship or train, or a place where a ship is tied up. The **birth** of someone or something is the act of it being born or created.

born, borne – To be **born** is to be brought into life. To be **borne** is to be accepted or carried. When fruit or flowers are **borne** by a plant, they are produced by it. If something is **borne** out, it is confirmed.

bough, bow – To **bow** is to bend your body or head, and a **bow** is an action where you bend your body or head. A **bough** is a branch of a tree.

brake, break – A **brake** is a device for slowing down, and to **brake** is to slow down by using this device. To **break** something is to change it so that it does not work or exist.

breath, breathe – **Breath**, without an 'e', is the noun, meaning 'air that is taken in by people or animals'. **Breathe**, with an 'e', is the verb meaning 'to take in air'.

canvas, canvass – **Canvas** is strong cloth. To **canvass** is to persuade people to vote a particular way or to find out their opinions about something.

caught, court – **Caught** means 'captured'. A **court** is an enclosed space, such as one used for legal cases or to play tennis.

cereal, serial – **Cereal** is food made from grain. A **serial** is something published or broadcast in a number of parts. **Serial** also describes other things that happen in a series.

cheetah, cheater – A **cheetah** is a kind of wild cat. A **cheater** is someone who cheats, for example by secretly breaking the rules of a game or an exam.

chord, cord – A **chord** is a group of three or more musical notes played together. **Cord** is strong thick string or electrical wire. Your vocal **cords** are folds in your throat, which are used to produce sound.

coarse, course – **Coarse** means 'rough' or 'rude'. A **course** is something that you go round (such as a *golf course*), or a series of things you do on a regular basis. **Course** is also used in the phrase *of course*.

complement, compliment – A **complement** is something that goes well with something else or completes it, and to **complement** something is to go well with it or complete it. A **compliment** is a remark expressing admiration, and to **compliment** (someone) on something is to express admiration for it.

confidant, confident – A **confidant** is a friend you tell secrets to. **Confident** means 'trusting' or 'self-assured'.

council, counsel – A **council** is a group of people elected to look after the affairs of an area. **Counsel** is advice and to **counsel** is to give advice.

currant, current – A **currant** is a small dried grape. A **current** is a flow of water, air or electricity. **Current** also means 'happening in the present'.

dairy, diary – **Dairy** products are foods made from milk. A **diary** is a small book in which you keep a record of appointments or record events.

decease, disease – The word **decease** means 'to die'. A **disease** is an illness or unhealthy condition.

defuse, diffuse – To **defuse** something is to make it less dangerous or tense. To **diffuse** something is to spread it or cause it to scatter.

dependant, dependent – **Dependant** is a noun meaning 'someone who receives financial support'. **Dependent** is an adjective describing someone who needs support.

desert, dessert – A **desert** is a region of land with little plant life. To **desert** someone is to abandon them. A **dessert** is sweet food served after the main course of a meal.

device, devise – **Device**, with a 'c', is the noun meaning 'an object invented for a particular purpose'. **Devise**, with an 's', is the verb meaning 'to think of and design a plan, system or machine'.

disc, disk – A **disc** is a flat round object. A **disc** can be a storage device used in computers, and also a piece of cartilage in your spine. **Disk** is the usual American spelling for all senses of this word, except in *compact disc*, which is always spelt with a 'c'.

discreet, discrete – If you are **discreet** you do not cause embarrassment about private matters. **Discrete** things are separate or distinct.

draft, draught – A **draft** is an early rough version of a speech or document. A **draught** is a current of cold air or an amount of liquid you swallow.

elicit, illicit – To **elicit** something, such as information, means 'to draw it out'. If something is **illicit** it is not allowed.

eligible, illegible – **Eligible** means 'suitable to be chosen for something'. If something is difficult to read, it is **illegible**.

---

emigrate, immigrate – If you **emigrate**, you leave a country to live somewhere else. If you **immigrate**, you enter a country to live there.

---

eminent, imminent – Someone who is **eminent** is well-known and respected. **Imminent** means 'about to happen'.

---

emit, omit – If something is **emitted**, it is let out. If you **omit** something, you leave it out.

---

enquire, inquire – These are alternative spellings of the same word. You can spell this word with an 'e' or an 'i', although the form **inquire** is more common.

---

ensure, insure – To **ensure** something happens is to make sure that it happens. To **insure** something is to take out financial cover against its loss. To **insure** against something is to do something in order to prevent it or protect yourself from it.

---

envelop, envelope – **Envelop** is the verb meaning 'to cover or surround'. **Envelope**, with an 'e' at the end, is the noun meaning 'a paper covering that holds a letter'.

---

exercise, exorcize – To **exercise** means to move energetically, and **exercise** is a period of energetic movement. To **exorcize** an evil spirit means 'to get rid of it'.

---

final, finale – **Final** means 'last of a series', and a **final** is the last game or contest in a series to decide the winner. A **finale**, with an 'e' at the end, is the finish of something,

especially the last part of a piece of music or a show.

---

gorilla, guerrilla – A **gorilla** is a large ape. A **guerrilla** is a member of a small unofficial army that is fighting an official army.

---

heir, air – An **heir** is someone who will inherit something. **Air** is the mixture of gases that we breathe.

---

heroin, heroine – **Heroin** is a powerful drug. The **heroine** of a story is the main female character in it.

---

idol, idle – An **idol** is a famous person who is worshipped by fans, or a picture or statue worshipped as a god. **Idle** means 'doing nothing'.

---

jewel, dual – A **jewel** is a precious stone. **Dual** means 'consisting of two parts'.

---

kerb, curb – A **kerb** is the raised area at the edge of a pavement. To **curb** something means to restrain it. In American English, **curb** is the spelling for both meanings.

---

leant, lent – **Leant** is the past tense of the verb lean. **Lent** is the past tense of the verb lend.

---

led, lead – **Led** is the past tense of the verb lead. **Lead**, when it is pronounced like **led**, is a soft metal, or the part of a pencil that makes a mark.

---

licence, license – **Licence**, ending in 'ce', is the noun. **License**, ending in 'se', is the verb. In American English, **license** is the spelling for both.

lose, loose – Something that is **loose** is not firmly held or not close-fitting. To **lose** something is not to have it any more, and to **lose** is also to be beaten in a game or a competition.

mat, matt – A **mat** is a covering for a floor. A **matt** colour has a dull (rather than shiny) appearance.

metre, meter – A **meter** is a device used to measure and record something. A **metre** is a metric unit of measurement. In American English, **meter** is the spelling for both these meanings.

morning, mourning – The **morning** is the first part of the day. **Mourning** is a form of the verb **mourn**, and means 'grieving for a dead person'.

net, nett – A **net** is an object or fabric with holes in it, such as a *net curtain*. The **nett** result of something is the final result after everything has been taken into consideration.

passed, past – **Passed** is the past tense of the verb **pass**. To go **past** something is to go beyond it. The **past** is the time before the present or describes things that existed before the present.

peace, piece – **Peace** is a state of calm and quiet. A **piece** is a part of something.

pedal, peddle – A **pedal** is a lever controlled with the foot, and to **pedal** something is to move its pedals. To **peddle** something is to sell it illegally.

personal, personnel – **Personal** means 'belonging or relating to a person'.

Personnel are the people employed to do a job.

pore, pour – If you **pore** over something, you study it carefully. A **pore** is also a tiny hole in the surface of your skin. To **pour** something is to let it flow out of a container, and if something **pours** it flows.

practice, practise – **Practice** is the noun meaning 'something that people do regularly' or 'something they do in order to get better at the activity'. **Practise** is the verb. In American English, **practise** is the spelling for both.

pray, prey – To **pray** means 'to speak to a god'. An animal's **prey** is the thing it hunts and kills to eat.

precede, proceed – Something that **precedes** another thing happens before it. If you **proceed**, you start or continue to do something.

principal, principle – **Principal** means 'main' or 'most important', and the **principal** of a school or college is the person in charge of it. A **principle** is a general rule, or a belief about the way you should behave.

program, programme – A **program** is a set of instructions for a computer, and you can **program** a computer. A **programme** is a plan or schedule, and also something on the television or radio. In American English, **program** is the spelling for both.

rain, reign, rein – **Rain** is water falling from the clouds. To **reign** is to rule a country or be the most noticeable feature of a situation. **Reins** are straps used to control a horse.

roll, role – To **roll** something means 'to make it move like a ball'. A **role** is a part that you play.

sceptic, septic – A **sceptic** is a person who expresses doubts. Something that is **septic** is infected by bacteria.

sight, site – **Sight** is the power to see, and a **sight** is something that you see. A **site** is a place with a special use.

stationary, stationery – **Stationary** means 'not moving'. **Stationery** is paper, pens and other writing equipment.

storey, story – A **storey** is a level in a building. A **story** is a description of events.

strait, straight – **Strait** means 'narrow', and is found in the words *straitjacket* and *strait-laced*. A **strait** is a narrow strip of water. **Straight** means 'not curved'.

symbol, cymbal – A **symbol** is something that represents another thing. A **cymbal** is a musical instrument.

through, threw – **Through** means 'going from one side to the other'. **Threw** is the past tense of the verb throw.

tide, tied – The **tide** is a change in the level of the sea on the shore. **Tied** is the past tense of the verb tie.

tire, tyre – To **tire** means 'to lose energy'. A **tyre** is the rubber ring round the wheel of a vehicle. In American English, **tire** is the spelling for both meanings.

vein, vain – **Vain** means 'proud of your looks or abilities'. **Veins** are tiny tubes in your body, through which your blood flows.

wander, wonder – To **wander** is to walk around in a casual way. To **wonder** is to speculate or enquire about something.

weather, whether – The **weather** is the conditions in the atmosphere (for example, rainy or sunny). **Whether** is a word used to introduce an alternative.

way, weigh – A **way** is a route or path, or a manner of doing something. To **weigh** something is to find out how heavy it is.

which, witch – **Which** is a word used to introduce a question, or to refer to a thing or things that have already been mentioned. A **witch** is a woman with magical powers.

wrap, rap – To **wrap** something means 'to put something around it', and a **wrap** is something that is folded round something else. A **rap** is a sharp blow, and **rap** is a style of music.

wring, ring – A **ring** is the sound made by a bell, and it is also a circle or enclosure. To **wring** something is to twist it.

Campbell, Colin, *Vocabulary Study Book*
(Garnet Education, 2007).

Carter, Ronald, Michael McCarthy and Anne O'Keefe, *From Corpus to Classroom*
(Cambridge University Press, 2007).

Ellis, Gail and Barbara Sinclair, *Learning to Learn English*
(Cambridge University Press, 2009).

McCarthy, Michael and Felicity O'Dell, *English Collocations in Use: Advanced*
(Cambridge University Press, 2008).

McCarthy, Michael, Anne O'Keefe and Steve Walsh, *Vocabulary Matrix*
(Heinle Cengage Teaching, 2010).

Zimmerman, Cheryl Boyd, *Word Knowledge*
(Oxford University Press, 2009).